MW01104901

Ark House Press
PO Box 1722, Port Orchard, WA 98366 USA
PO Box 1321, Mona Vale NSW 1660 Australia
PO Box 318 334, West Harbour, Auckland 0661 New Zealand
arkhousepress.com

© 2017 Gordon Moore

Cataloguing in Publication Data:
Title: Ascent
ISBN: 9780648084556 (pbk.)
Subjects: Christian Living
Other Authors/Contributors: Moore, Gordon

Design and layout by C3 Church Bridgeman Downs www.c3bd.com

ASCENT

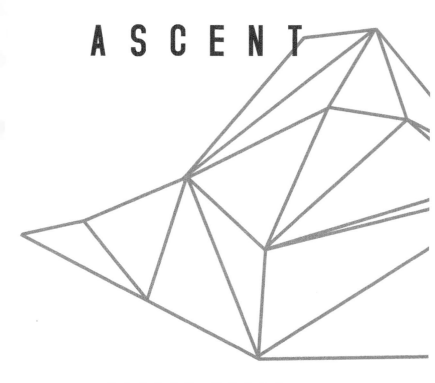

GORDON MOORE
DEVOTIONAL JOURNEY OF FAITH

"HIGHER GROUND"
Johnson Oatman, Jr

I'm pressing on the upward way,
New heights I'm gaining every day;
Still praying as I onward bound,
"Lord, plant my feet on higher ground."

Lord, lift me up, and let me stand
By faith on Canaan's tableland;
A higher plane than I have found,
Lord, plant my feet on higher ground.

My heart has no desire to stay
Where doubts arise and fears dismay;
Though some may dwell where these abound,
My prayer, my aim, is higher ground.

I want to live above the world,
Though Satan's darts at me are hurled;
For faith has caught the joyful sound,
The song of saints on higher ground.

I want to scale the utmost height
And catch a gleam of glory bright;
But still I'll pray till rest I've found,
"Lord, lead me on to higher ground."

INTRODUCTION

The fifteen "Songs of Ascent" have always
been a spiritual anthem for me because they
describe our pilgrim journey of faith so well. Over the
years, I have found myself reading them, meditating
on them, often quoting them and finding spiritual
strength and stamina for my journey of ascent into
God.

This book is a devotional journey of ascent into God's
higher life for us.

These 'songs' outline the progressive, upward and
onward journey of faith into the high calling of God in
Christ Jesus for all believers.

"Brethren, I count not myself to have apprehended:
but this one thing I do,
forgetting those things which are behind,
and reaching forward to those things which are
before,
I press toward the mark for the prize of the high
calling of God in Christ Jesus."
Philippians 3:13-14

Each Psalm presents a Spiritual truth that we must
understand and embrace in order to progress to the
next level in our faith and experience with God.

All through the New Testament, the life of the believer is presented as a progressive, upward and ever increasing journey.

> *"Be diligent in these things.*
> *Give yourself wholly to them,*
> *that your **progress** may be revealed to all."*
> *1Timothy 4:15 (WEB)*

For example, in the parable of the Sower in Matthew Chapter 13, we could view each type of 'soil', or 'ground', as separate hearts or people. However, upon closer investigation, we also discover that the 'four hearts' can be viewed as the progressive, unfolding experience that is common to every believer in Christ.

In reality, the "Good Ground" has encountered every 'condition' of "wayside, rocks and weeds" in its journey to become "Good Ground." Specifically, this means:

a.   The fallow, unplowed, abandoned, hard soil of the "Wayside"
b.   The stony and shallow soil of the "Rocky Ground"
c.   The weedy, uncared for and neglected soil of the "Thorny Ground"

So what makes "Good Ground" good ground? "Good Ground" is the result of constant plowing, tilling, weeding and caring for the ground. In most instances, it takes years for a farmer to produce

"Good Ground," and so it is with us.

We are called to journey ever upwards, ever ascending, ever progressing and discovering our "high calling in Christ Jesus."

The path of ascent is not a straight path. It is a mountain climb with many twists and turns along our journey up Mount Zion to the House of God.

Sometimes it doesn't feel or look like we're making progress. We may need to go sideways and even backwards in order to negotiate valleys and obstacles to make progress but, because our eyes are fixed on the prize, Christ Jesus himself, we hold constant in faith, we keep moving, we keep turning up, so that we can find a way to progress, to grow and ever ascend in our journey of faith.

When we first trusted in Christ, we were responding as sinners to God's work for us in Christ. After we trust in Christ we are to be like the diligent farmer, tilling our hearts through the obedience of faith, activating God's work in us through the power of the Holy Spirit.

"…Work out your own salvation with
fear and trembling,
for it is God who works in you both to will
and to do His good pleasure."
Philippians 2:12-13

God has a far bigger idea about us than we could imagine!

"But as it is written, eye has not seen, nor ear heard, neither have entered into the heart of man, the things which God has prepared for them that love Him."
1 Corinthians 2:9

We are not destined to live for eighty-plus years on the earth and that's it! We were created by God to live forever in relationship and fellowship with Him – to share His glory!

There are two things that I am very, very glad about:

Firstly, **I'm glad God is FOR ME and not against me!**

"What then shall we say about these things?
If God is for us, who can be against us?
*Indeed, he who did not spare his own Son, but gave him up for us all – how will he not also, **along with him, freely give us all things**?"*
Romans 8:31-32 (NET)

Secondly, **I'm glad God's thoughts toward me are GOOD!**

*"**For I know the thoughts that I think toward you,
says the LORD**,
thoughts of peace, and not of evil,
to give you an expected end."*
Jeremiah 29:11

*"For I know what I have planned for you',
says the Lord.
'I have plans to prosper you, not to harm you.
I have plans to give you a future filled with hope."*
Jeremiah 29:11 (NET)

God's knowledge, calling, and love of me **PRECEDE**
my existence!

*"Before I formed you in the belly I knew you;
and before you came forth out of the womb
I sanctified you,
and **I ordained you** a prophet unto the nations."*
Jeremiah 1:5

*"Your eyes did see my substance,
yet being unperfect;
and in Your book all my members were written,
which in continuance were fashioned,
when as yet there was none of them."*
Psalm 139:16

*"**Your eyes saw me** when I was inside the womb.*
All the days ordained for me were recorded in your
*scroll **before one of them came into existence**."*
Psalm 139:16 (NET)

God's thoughts towards us are as countless as the
sand on the seashore! Imagine that!

*"**How difficult it is for me to fathom your***
thoughts about me, O God!
How vast is their sum total!
If I tried to count them, they would outnumber the
grains of sand.
Even if I finished counting them,
I would still have to contend with you."
Psalm 139:17-18 (NET)

The Psalmist tells us that God's thoughts toward us
even outnumber the grains of sand on the seashore.
What imagery! Our Heavenly Father is thinking
about us all of the time! He never stops thinking
about us and they are not thoughts of condemnation
and judgement, they are thoughts of love, hope and
destiny!

Historically, these fifteen Psalms were sung by the
Israelites on their way up to the House of God three
times a year for the feasts in Jerusalem.

"And it shall come to pass in the last days,
that the mountain of the Lord's house shall be

11

established in the top of the mountains,
and shall be exalted above the hills;
and all nations shall flow unto it.
And many people shall go and say,
*Come, and let us **go up***
to the mountain of the Lord,
to the house of the God of Jacob;
and he will teach us of his ways,
and we will walk in his paths:
for out of Zion shall go forth the law,
and the word of the LORD from Jerusalem."
Isaiah 2:2-3

The Psalms can be seen as three stages of progress and growth in faith:

Psalms 120 - 124	Psalms 125 - 129	Psalms 130 - 134
ENTERING	ESTABLISHING	ENDURING
BIRTHING	DISCIPLING	MATURING
Repentance Faith Fellowship Service Testimony	Trust Sowing + Reaping Building + Keeping Faithfulness Perseverance	Hope Humility Obedience Unity Blessing
"Children"	"Young Men" (Sons)	"Fathers"

Tradition suggests that there were probably fifteen steps up into the Temple and that each Psalm was sung on each of the steps as a form of preparation of the faithful as they gathered to worship.

"On the fifteen steps which led into the women's court, corresponding with fifteen Songs of Degrees, stood the Levites, with their musical instruments and sang." (m.Sukkah 5:4-5)

Furthermore, each Psalm was a declaration and testimony of the calling and progressive nature of the Israelites' deliverance and restoration as a people out of slavery and confusion in Babylon to love, hope and joy in Mount Zion, the City of God.

The highest calling and privilege for the Israelites is expressed in the final Song of Ascent:

"Behold, bless the Lord, all you servants of the Lord,
who by night stand in the house of the Lord.
Lift up your hands in the sanctuary,
and bless the Lord.
The Lord that made heaven and earth
bless you out of Zion.
Psalm 134:1-3

And so it is with us: our highest calling and privilege is to stand in God's House as servants blessing our God.

The Ascent was the journey from distress to blessing.

It was the journey from being strangers in a foreign

land to being servants of the Lord in the Promised Land.

It was the journey from servitude to servanthood.

It was the journey from sorrow to joy.

It was the journey from poverty to prosperity.

It was the journey from despair to hope.

We too, are on a similar journey of Ascent. Our 'spiritual journey' to maturity in Christ is akin to the Israelites.

We also begin with, *"In my distress I called to the Lord" (Psalm 120:1).*

We journey from the "strange land" of bondage to sin and spiritual confusion and ascend to… *"bless the Lord, all you servants of the Lord who by night stand in the house of the Lord." (Psalm 134)*

The miracle that God performs in us is to transform us from being lost souls wandering in a strange land, to becoming servants of God standing secure as "pillars in God's House," the Church.

Born again, transformed, mature, fully equipped and reigning in Christ – this is God's vision of us in Christ!

*"Who has delivered us
from the power of darkness,
and has translated us
into the kingdom of his dear Son...*

*Which is Christ in you, the hope of glory:
Whom we preach, warning every man,
and teaching every man in all wisdom;
that we may present every man
perfect in Christ Jesus."
Colossians 1:13, 27-28*

Reader's Note:
I have included space for you to journal your own meditation notes and list your prayers and actions at the end of each Psalm. Selah.

My prayer is that you will also be inspired to do the upward, onward and progressive journey with God through these wonderful Psalms... "The Songs of Ascent."

Gordon Moore
AUTHOR

CHAPTER 1

REPENTANCE

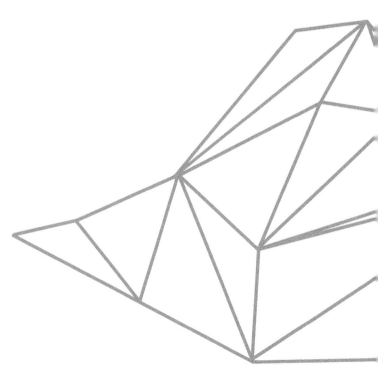

P S A L M   1 2 0
" I   N E E D   G O D "

"In my distress I cried to the Lord, and He heard me."
Psalm 120:1

The Psalmist begins his ascent upwards with a cry of desperation..."**IN MY DISTRESS**"

This is where we must all begin...at 'rock bottom.' When we are self-assured, stubborn and content with our lot in life, we can never start our journey of ascent into God!

HOW DO WE ARRIVE AT THIS PLACE OF UNDERSTANDING?

Like the Psalmist, we must come to a revelation regarding the evil predicament of our circumstances. We need deliverance from:
* "Lying lips"
* "A Deceitful Tongue"
* "Meshech"
* "Kedar"
* "War"

The Psalmist is confessing his loathing of his condition away from God.

He finds himself in trouble and unrest, amongst 'lying' and 'war', because he is dwelling in 'Meshech' and 'Kedah,' far away from God's House.

The Psalmist uses these two people to metaphorically illustrate his position far away from God and God's House, dwelling among barbarous, uncivilized people.

"Meshech", "who is drawn by force", was traditionally understood as fierce and distant, and "Kedah", who was the son of Ishmael, persecuted and ridiculed Isaac the heir of Abraham.

He wants out of this trouble, this confusion and this godless environment. He has begun his ascent in the decision of his heart.

I can still vividly remember my beginning with God. As a new convert, I desperately wanted out of my old life and to be in Christ's new life! This desperation for Christ is the beginning of salvation in us.

The first revelation is the realisation that we have been **sold a lie** and that we are **LIVING A LIE!**

This has been the situation from the beginning:

"Now the serpent was more subtle
than any beast of the field
which the Lord God had made.
And he said unto the woman, yes, has God said,

you shall not eat of every tree of the garden?"
Genesis 3:1

The devil, "**the father of lies**", has ensnared us with no apparent way of escape.

"You are of your father the devil,
and the lusts of your father ye will do.
*He was a **murderer** from the beginning, and abode*
*not in the truth, because **there is no truth in him**.*
When he speaks a lie, he speaks of his own:
*for **he is a liar, and the father of it**."*
John 8:44

The deeper we go listening to 'the lie' of the devil, the blinder we become to the truth of God.

*"In whom the god of this world has **blinded the***
***minds of them who believe not**,*
lest the light of the glorious gospel of Christ,
who is the image of God, should shine unto them."
2 Corinthians 4:4

So is there no way of escape? That in itself is a lie! For God has provided our escape through the Lord Jesus Christ!

"Our soul has escaped as a bird
out of the snare of the fowlers;
the snare is broken, and we are escaped!"
Psalm 124:7

*"The thief (devil) comes not, but for to **steal**,
and to **kill**, and to **destroy**:
I am come that they might have life,
and that they might have it more abundantly."*
John 10:10

We must come to a place of rejecting the '**lie of the devil**' and embracing the '**truth of God**'. God calls us to be **light dwellers**; living in the light of His presence where there is no darkness, fear or deceit.

WE MAKE THE CHANGE, *"If we walk in the light…"* *(1 John 1:7)*.

Through **REPENTANCE**.

'Repentance' is a change of mind about our circumstances.

Before repentance, we **chose our sin or our own way**. Now we have a change of mind (through repentance) and **choose righteousness**.

Repentance is taking God's side against ourselves. We decide that God was right all along and that we have been following our own vanity and foolishness.

Repentance is a change in attitude.

We begin to be 'over' the fleeting "pleasures of sin" and now realize how negative and destructive our sin is. The truly repentant heart becomes desperate to please God.

*"For the **wages of sin is death**;*
but the gift of God is eternal life
through Jesus Christ our Lord."
Romans 6:23

"There is a way which seems right unto a man,
*but **the end thereof are the ways of death**."*
Proverbs 14:12

Repentance is a change in action resulting in a complete turn from actions of sin to actions of righteousness.

Repentance is a deep, emotional remorse about our sin, our disobedience and our separation from God. This "Godly sorrow" activates us and moves us to repentance.

"For Godly sorrow produces repentance leading to
Salvation, not to be regretted;
but the sorrow of the world produces death"
2 Corinthians 7:10

"Do you not know that to whom you present yourself
slaves to obey,

you are that one's slaves when you obey,
whether of sin leading to death,
or of obedience leading to righteousness."
Romans 6:16

"I'm in distress" because of my trouble and unrest. I'm dwelling amongst Meshech and Kedah (Ishmael), with bondage and conflict, fighting, with no peace. But I realize I have a problem...I can't save myself!

"I NEED GOD!" IS MY DESPERATE CRY.

THIS IS THE BEGINNING OF OUR JOURNEY OF ASCENT INTO GOD.

"Who shall ascend the hill of the Lord?
And who shall stand in his holy place?
He who has clean hands and a pure heart,
who does not lift up his soul
to what is false and does not swear deceitfully.
He will receive blessing from the Lord and
righteousness from the God of his salvation."
Psalm 24:3-5

PRAYER

Lord Jesus, I open the door of my heart
and invite you in.
I repent and turn from sin
and everything that displeases you.
Forgive me and make me clean on the inside,
make me a child of God.
I promise to follow you and serve you all my days
In Jesus name,
AMEN

MEDITATIONS:

ACTIONS:

CHAPTER 2

FAITH

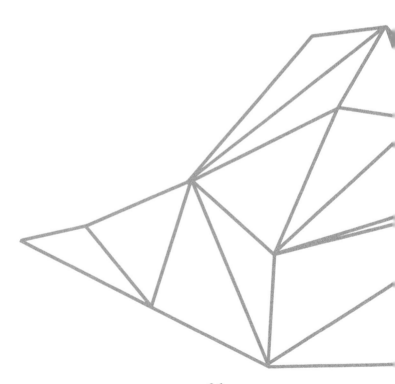

PSALM 121

"I LOOK TO GOD"

"I will lift my eyes to the hills - Where does my help come from? My help comes from the Lord, who made heaven and earth."
Psalm 121:1-2

A clear shift has occurred in the heart of the Psalmist from being in a place of distress, and looking out to the hills and "to the Lord."

It's not enough to know that we are in distress and things aren't working out. It's not enough to feel sorry, or even guilty about our sins; we have to find the Lord in our circumstances. If we don't, we can become like Esau who couldn't, *"find a place for repentance, though he sought it diligently with tears."* Hebrews 12:17

It doesn't matter where we look – to men, hills, books or counsellors. We are destined to disappointment if we don't look to the Lord!

We begin our ascent by repenting and acknowledging our sin and bondage, and as we make that shift and receive forgiveness and cleansing by Christ, our eyes are opened to the Lord. This is 'the look of faith'.

Our sins that blinded us have been removed through repentance and now we can see.

"Looking unto Jesus
the author and finisher of our faith."
Hebrews 12:2

"And as Moses lifted up the serpent in the wilderness,
even so must the Son of man be lifted up:
That whoever believes in Him should not perish,
but have eternal life."
John 3:14-15

THE DEEPER THE REPENTANCE
THE HIGHER THE FAITH

This is no longer the 'look of desperation;' this is the 'look of revelation.'

Before we see the Lord, we only see our problems, our sins, our circumstances and our anxiety.
Now we see the God who is above all and is THE ANSWER to our every need! This is the 'good news.'

We not only see our problems; we now see the Lord as our provider, our helper and our protector through faith.

"What shall we then say to these things?
If God be for us, who can be against us?

He that spared not his own Son,
but delivered him up for us all,
how shall he not with him
also freely give us all things?"
Romans 8:31-32

Knowing that the Lord is for me and not against me is the 'faith revelation.' Faith changes everything – the way we see things, the way we feel, the way we act and the way we respond!

Without God keeping us, we are exposed to the three dangers of life:

a.   **'Stumbling'** - "foot to be moved" (Psalm 121:3)
        -      We stumble when we don't find a sure and steadfast path to walk in. We must daily walk in the way of God's Word.

"And make straight paths for your feet,
lest that which is lame be turned out of the way;
but let it rather be healed."
Hebrews 12:13

b.   **'Sunstroke'** - "sun smite you by day" (Psalm 121:6)
        -      Sunstroke can smite us as we walk through difficult situations and when our faith is tested. 'Sunstroke' is a metaphor for testing, trials and adversity. Our roots must be found deep in Christ alone so we

can have the capacity to draw sustenance
from Christ in trying and testing times.

"And when the sun was up, they were scorched;
and because they had no root, they withered away.
Yet he has not root in himself, but endures for a while:
for when tribulation or persecution arises because of
the word, by and by he is offended."
Matthew 13:6,21

c.   **'Moonstroke'** - "moon smite you by night"
         (Psalm 121:6)
         -       The Psalmist was well acquainted with
                 the 'lunacy of worry and anxiety' that often
                 comes unwanted in the night seasons
                 flooding our minds and emotions:

" I am weary with my groaning.
Every night I flood my bed.
I drench my couch with my tears.
My eye wastes away because of grief.
It grows old because of all my adversaries."
Psalm 6:6-7

The apostle Paul discovered the secret to overcoming
anxiety by looking to the Lord in prayer:

"In nothing be anxious, but in everything,
by prayer and petition with thanksgiving,
let your requests be made known to God.
And the peace of God, which surpasses all

understanding, will guard your hearts
and your thoughts in Christ Jesus."
Philippians 4:6-7

WORRY IS LIKE A ROCKING CHAIR,
IT GIVES YOU SOMETHING TO DO,
BUT IT WON'T GET YOU ANYWHERE.

The Psalmist now reveals the God who he sees
by faith and lists **eight times** that the Lord is his
"KEEPER, SHADE, PRESERVER AND GUARDIAN".

"He will not suffer your foot to be moved:
*he that **keeps** you will not slumber.*
*Behold, he that **keeps** Israel*
shall neither slumber nor sleep.
*The Lord is your **keeper**:*
*the Lord is your **shade** upon your right hand.*
The sun shall not smite you by day,
nor the moon by night.
*The Lord shall **preserve** you from all evil:*
*he shall **preserve** your soul.*
*The Lord shall **preserve** your going out and your*
coming in from this time forth,
and even for evermore."
Psalm 121:3-8

Our lives become messed up when we continue to
look in the wrong direction. Repentance clears the
way for us to see clearly and look to God by faith.

"MY HELP COMES FROM THE LORD."

MEDITATIONS:

ACTIONS:

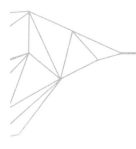

CHAPTER 3

WORSHIP & FELLOWSHIP

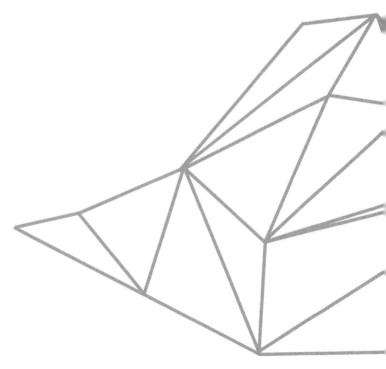

PSALM 122

"MAKING GOD'S HOUSE MY PRIORITY"

"I was glad when they said to me,
let us go to the House of the Lord."
Psalm 122:1

Building the House of God is very important to God. The Scriptures present Jesus singing in the midst of the church (Hebrews 2:12). The company of the heroes of faith cheers the church on (Hebrews 12:1).

Psalm 122 is the third Psalm of the 'Songs of Ascent.'

These fifteen Psalms reveal the **progressive journey** upwards to the '**higher life in Christ**'.

Psalm 120 is where we begin:
REPENTANCE - "I need God".

Psalm 121 is where we relocate our hearts to total abandonment to God:
FAITH - "I trust in God".

Psalm 122 is when we understand God's priority:
COMMITMENT - "I make God's House central to my life".

This is God's **PRIORITY** for our lives, but this is not

an empty, or futile request by God. Making God's House central in our lives is God's priority!

God has placed the church to be the source of blessing for us. This is His priority.

> *"The Lord bless you out of Zion."*
> *Psalm 128:5*

The Psalmist jubilantly declares his '**GOD PRIORITY**.'

> *"I was glad when they said to me,*
> *let us go to the House of the Lord."*
> *Psalm 122:1*

The call of God to 'ascend' is to commit to a **life long priority** of **worshipping and fellowshipping in God's House, the church**.

The Psalmist is immediately filled with joy because he discovers he's not the only one who has set God's House as their priority.

When he was lost in his sin, he felt alone and abandoned. When he discovered repentance and faith, his eyes were opened. He discovered God's House and he found his family of faith!

> "I was glad when **THEY** said to me..."

Who are "**THEY**"?

"THEY" are the…

'ONES WHO GO TO THE HOUSE OF GOD!'

*"Surely goodness and mercy
shall follow me all the days of my life:
and I **will dwell in the house of the LORD for ever**."*
Psalm 23:6

*"My soul longs, yes, even f**aints
for the courts of the LORD**:
my heart and my flesh cry out for the living God."*
Psalm 84:2

"THEY" resonate together because of their deep
desire for God.

"THEY" realize that this deep longing for God is not
found on their own or in isolation.

"THEY" recognize the blessings of being in God's
House together.

*"For a day in your courts is better than a thousand.
I had rather be a doorkeeper in the house of my God,
than to dwell in the tents of wickedness."*
Psalm 84:10

Our Creator God's intention was never to do life
alone, and especially our 'spiritual life'.

The only way we can truly grow and develop in God is to be **built together in God's House!**

The Apostle Paul put it this way…

"Now therefore you are no longer strangers and
foreigners, but fellow citizens with the saints,
*and of the **household of God**;*
and are built upon the foundation
of the apostles and prophets,
Jesus Christ himself being the chief corner stone;
*in whom all the **building fitly framed together grows***
unto an holy temple in the Lord:
***in whom you also are built together** for an*
habitation of God through the Spirit."
Ephesians 2:19-22

God's House, the church, is the place of connection, health, growth, and development!

The Psalmist lists five reasons why it is important to be in God's House.

The Five 'T's' of God's House:

1. TOGETHER (Psalm 122:3)
The Church is unified, one body, one people.

*"For as **the body is one**, and has many members,*
*and all the members of that **one body**, being many,*
*are **one body**: so also is Christ.*

38

*For by **one Spirit** are we all baptized into **one body**,*
whether we be Jews or Gentiles,
whether we be bond or free;
*and have been all made to drink into **one Spirit**.*
For the body is not one member, but many."
1 Corinthians 12:12-14

Our responsibility is not to **GET** the unity, but to **KEEP** the unity we already have in Christ.

*"Endeavoring to **KEEP THE UNITY OF THE SPIRIT***
in the bond of peace."
Ephesians 4:3

2. TRIBES (Psalm 122:4)
When we become '**House of God Dwellers**,' we leave behind our backgrounds, circumstances and opinions. Through our attendance, we declare that we are united as one people and tribe in God!

"Now I beseech you, brethren,
by the name of our Lord Jesus Christ,
*that you all **speak the same thing**,*
*and that there be **no divisions** among you;*
*but that you be **perfectly joined together** in the*
***same mind** and in the **same judgment**."*
1 Corinthians 1:10

"There is neither Jew nor Greek,
there is neither bond nor free,
there is neither male nor female:

*for **you are all one in Christ Jesus**."*
Galatians 3:28

*"What is true architecturally is also true socially,
for the sentence continues, "to which the tribes
ascend, all God's tribes." In worship all the different
tribes functioned as a single people in harmonious
relationship."*
Eugene Petersen

3. TESTIMONY (Psalm 122:4)

*"Your **testimonies** also are my delight
and my counsellors."*
Psalm 119:24

*"I thought on my ways,
and turned my feet unto your testimonies."*
Psalm 119:59

*"The **law** of the LORD is perfect,
converting the soul:
**the testimony of the LORD is sure,
making wise the simple**.
The **statutes** of the LORD are right,
rejoicing the heart:
the **commandment** of the LORD is pure,
enlightening the eyes."*
Psalm 19:7-8

"The testimony of the Lord is sure...."

We can know with certainty that His testimony is plain, decided and infallible.

God bears his testimony against sin, and on behalf of righteousness, he testifies of our fall and of our restoration in Christ.

"Making wise the simple."
Humble and teachable minds receive the Word of God and are made wise unto salvation.

As a law or plan, the Word of God converts, and then as a testimony, it instructs us. It is not enough for us to be converts, we must continue to be disciples – those taught in the Word of God.

**IT IS ONLY IN THE CONTEXT
OF FELLOWSHIP AND WORSHIP IN GOD'S
HOUSE THAT WE UNDERSTAND AND
COMPREHEND THE FULL UNDERSTANDING OF
OUR FAITH AS GOD BEARS TESTIMONY TO US
AND REVEALS HIS FULLNESS.
THE FULLNESS OF CHRIST
IS FOUND IN GOD'S HOUSE.**

*"But **WE** have the mind of Christ."*
1Corinthians 2:16

*"And he gave some, apostles;
and some, prophets; and some, evangelists;
and some, pastors and teachers;*

For the perfecting of the saints*,*
for the work of the ministry,
for the edifying of the body of Christ:
Till we all come in the unity of the faith,
and of the knowledge of the Son of God,
unto a perfect man, unto the measure of the
stature of the fullness of Christ*."*
Ephesians 4:11-13

"The Testimony of Israel" in the Old Testament
was the Ark of the Covenant, which testified to the
Israelites of their escape from slavery, their wilderness
journey and their possession of the land of Promise.

The Israelites were commanded to appear in
Jerusalem for two purposes:
a.   To worship God
b.   To hear the Word of God preached

It's the same today! God's plan is simple and it never
changes.

We are admonished to appear in Church as the
Saints, gathered and assembled for two purposes:
a.   To worship God
b.   To hear the Word of God preached

4. THRONES (Psalm 122:5)
In worship we are **CENTERED** on God's decisions,
God's directions and God's priorities.

We are presented with God's *"thrones (which) are set for judgement."*

We are gathered in God's House to be brought into connection with spiritual leadership.

We are gathered to be submitted to spiritual authority.

We are gathered to be knitted into the "Apostle's doctrine" and teaching.

> *"And they **continued steadfastly in the apostles' doctrine and fellowship**,*
> *and in breaking of bread, and in prayers."*
> *Acts 2:42*

There is simply no other setting or context where this is better achieved but in God's House. When we gather for worship and fellowship, we discover the Word of God is everywhere, **beginning with the command of Scripture to come to God's House to obey God's Word.**

> *"Not forsaking our own assembling together,*
> *as is the manner (custom) of some,*
> *but exhorting one another; and so much the more, as you see the Day approaching."*
> *Hebrews 10:25*

*Let the word of Christ dwell in you richly in all wisdom;
teaching and admonishing one another
in psalms and hymns and spiritual songs,
singing with grace in your hearts to the Lord."
Colossians 3:16*

*"Day by day, continuing steadfastly with one accord in
the temple, and breaking bread at home,
they took their food with gladness and
singleness of heart,
praising God, and having favor with all the people.
The Lord added to the assembly day by day those
who were being saved."
Acts 2:46-47*

In the church gathered, the Word of God is:
- **Exemplified** in the **lives** of our **spiritual fathers and mothers**
- **Heard** in the **words** of the **faithful**
- **Articulated** in the **songs of worship and praise**
- **Expressed** in the **sermons** and **teaching**
- **Confirmed** in the **prayers of the saints**
- **Portrayed** in the **worship** and **offerings** of the **congregation**
- **Shared** during the **fellowship and hospitality of the members**
- **Released to the world** through the **empowered Saints** when scattered

5. THANKS (Psalm 122:4)
The reason we keep returning to God's House is
GRATITUDE. How can we not come to God with
hearts full of **THANKSGIVING** for His goodness and
blessing in our lives?

> *"What shall I render unto the LORD*
> *for all his benefits toward me?*
> *I will take the cup of salvation,*
> *and call upon the name of the LORD.*
> *I will pay my vows unto the LORD now in the*
> *presence of all his people."*
> *Psalm 116:12-14*

WHERE ARE THE NINE?

"And one of them, when he saw that he was healed,
turned back, *and with a loud voice* ***glorified God,***
And fell down on his face at his feet,
giving him thanks:
and he was a Samaritan.
And Jesus answering said,
were there not ten cleansed?
But where are the nine?
Were there not any found who returned to give
glory to God, *except this foreigner?*
And he said unto him, Arise, go your way:
your faith has made you whole."
Luke 15:17-19

God is asking us today...

"Where are the nine?"
"Where are the saved ones?"
"Where are the forgiven ones?"
"Where are the healed ones?"
"Where are the blessed ones?"

It is sad to see many believers today out of God's House, trying to do their faith journey alone. "I don't have to be in church to be a Christian," they protest, not realizing that the journey of faith is a corporate one.

It begins with a personal revelation through repentance and faith, but is worked out through commitment and connection to God's House, the church.

"For by one Spirit are we all baptized into one body,
whether we be Jews or Gentiles,
whether we be bond or free;
and have been all made to drink into one Spirit.
For the body is not one member, but many.
If the foot shall say, Because I am not the hand,
I am not of the body;
is it therefore not of the body?
And if the ear shall say, Because I am not the eye,
I am not of the body;
is it therefore not of the body?
If the whole body were an eye,

where were the hearing?
If the whole were hearing, where were the smelling?
But now hath God set the members every one of
them in the body, as it hath pleased him.
And if they were all one member,
where were the body?
But now are they many members, yet but one body.
And the eye cannot say unto the hand,
I have no need of you:
nor again the head to the feet, I have no need of you."
1 Corinthians 12:13-21

While it is true that you don't have to be in church to **become** a Christian, you cannot **be** a Christian without being in church.

Show me a Christian who is not in church and I'll show you an unhealthy Christian.

The authenticity of our love for God is very easily measured by our gladness for being in God's House.

I have observed over the years that the first move by a backslidden Christian is to stop being in church.

"I was glad when they said to me, "let us go to the
House of the Lord!"
Psalm 122:1

AUTHENTIC SPIRITUALITY DOES NOT HAPPEN ALONE

"But as for me,
because of your great faithfulness
I will enter your house;
I will bow down toward your holy temple
*as I **worship you**."*
Psalm 5:8

The Blessings of the 'House of God Dwellers' –

God wants to bless us, to add value and not disappoint us.

"For the Scripture says, "Whoever believes in him will not be disappointed."
Romans 10:11

Psalm 122 ends with declaring the two blessings that come upon us as '**HOUSE OF GOD DWELLERS**.'

When we put God's priorities of fellowship and worship first, God promises we will receive:

1. **PEACE** – no more war, lies or turmoil, but peace and well being of heart.
2. **PROSPERITY** – a life of joy, success and progress.

The first word in the Psalmist's conclusion is "**PRAY**."

**As a result of committing to a life of worship and
fellowship in God's House,
our hearts will overflow in a life of prayer!**

Worship and fellowship in God's House is the
foundation and the catalyst from which our life in the
world is set up. We are emboldened and strengthened
in God's House to go out into all of the world!

> *"Blessed are they that dwell in Your House:
> they will be still praising you. Selah."*
> *Psalm 84:4*

When God's House, the church, is at the center in
our lives, we have the right perspective.... **GOD'S
PERSPECTIVE!**

We have made God's House our priority!

> *"I was glad when they said unto me,
> let us go into the house of the LORD".*
> *Psalm 122:1*

MEDITATIONS:

ACTIONS:

INTERLUDE

These first three songs of Ascent are the 'ASCENT FOUNDATIONS'.

Repentance - Faith - Fellowship

Without them, our journey of ascent cannot begin.

Now that these truths are firmly set in our lives through obedience as a solid foundation, our feet will not be moved, and our journey onwards and upwards commences. SELAH!

"Therefore leaving the discussion of elementary principles of Christ,
Let us go on to maturity not laying again the foundation of repentance from dead works and of faith towards God.
And this we will do if God permits."
Hebrews 6:1-3

CHAPTER 4

WATCHING
& WAITING

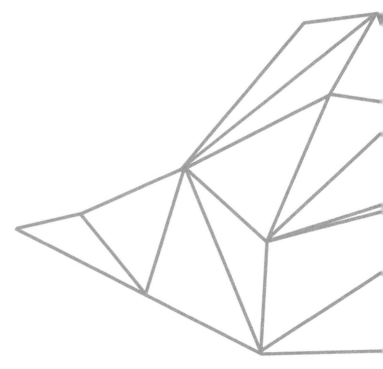

PSALM 123
"I AM GOD'S SERVANT"

"To you I do lift up my eyes,
you who sit in the heavens.
Behold, as the eyes of servants
look to the hand of their master,
as the eyes of a maid to the hand of her mistress;
so our eyes look to the Lord, our God,
until he has mercy on us."
Psalm 123:1-2

The next step in our journey of faith is a critical one…
SERVANTHOOD.

"No servant can serve two masters:
for either he will hate the one, and love the other;
or else he will hold to the one, and despise the other.
You cannot serve God and mammon."
Luke 16:13

"And he said unto them, the kings of the Gentiles
exercise lordship over them;
and they that exercise authority upon them
are called benefactors.
But you shall not be so:
but he that is greatest among you,
let him be as the younger;
*and **he that is chief, as he that serves**."*
Luke 22:25-26

Becoming a servant of God is not a matter of compulsion or servitude, but rather the result of **revelation**. This understanding causes a radical shift in our mindset and behaviour because we are living from a new perspective, a new posture and attitude of **humility**:

*"**Let this mind be in you,
which was also in Christ Jesus**:
who, being in the form of God,
thought it not robbery to be equal with God:
but made himself of no reputation,
and took upon him the form of a servant,
and was made in the likeness of men:
And being found in fashion as a man,
he humbled himself,
and became obedient unto death,
even the death of the cross."
Philippians 2:5-8*

Our eyes are now looking to the Lord:
For His **instruction**,
For His **command**,
For His **direction**,
For His **request**,
For His **prompting**,
For His **leading**.

"Behold, as the **eyes** of **servants**
look unto the hand of their masters,

*and as the **eyes** of a **maiden**
unto the hand of her mistress;
so **our eyes wait upon the LORD our God**."*
Psalm 123:2

How things are changed! In the beginning of his journey of ascent, the Psalmist is **enquiring out of desperation**…

"WHERE DOES MY HELP COME FROM?"

He is "looking to the hills" and discovers...

"MY HELP COMES FROM THE LORD!"

But now he declares in faith...

"UNTO YOU I LIFT MY EYES,
O YOU WHO DWELL IN THE HEAVENS."
Psalm 123:1

He is looking to the 'Heaven dwelling God'. His look is no longer natural or out of need; his look is now spiritual, out of faith.

> *"**Looking unto Jesus**
> the author and finisher of our faith."*
> *Hebrews 12:2*

Again, this is the '**LOOK OF FAITH**,'

"For they that are after the flesh
*do **mind the things of the flesh**;*
but they that are after the Spirit
*the **things of the Spirit.***
For to be carnally minded is death;
*but t**o be spiritually minded is life and peace**.*
Because the carnal mind is enmity against God:
for it is not subject to the law of God,
neither indeed can be."
Romans 8:5-7

Once we have ascended to this view of faith (for our faith is in Christ alone as His servant), we now are in a constant position of **waiting, anticipating and expecting**. We are '**WAITING ON GOD**.'

To be a '**SERVANT**.' we have to learn how to '**WAIT**.' The heart of the servant is geared to the wishes, commands and needs of their master. Acting under the direction and approval of our Lord is our only concern.

"I know of only one danger:
not to be in the centre of God's will."
Corrie Ten Boom

*"But they that **wait upon the Lord***
shall renew their strength;
they shall mount up with wings as eagles;
they shall run, and not be weary;

and they shall walk, and not faint."
Isaiah 40:31

"WAIT" means to "look for (eagerly), hope, expect, linger for, tarry". (H6960 – Strong's Concordance)

Waiting is no easy task in our culture! **We live in a 'culture of rush'** - constantly moving, changing and restless. We demand the **instant**, the **now**, and the world delivers!

If you're like me, you cannot stand waiting! Have you ever dropped off your spouse at a shopping centre to hear, "I'll meet you here in an hour"... two hours later!

It's the same when we visit the doctor. Notice how they call the seating area the 'waiting room,' not reception, because you're going to wait!

Even in the church world we can be in a rush, imbibing the 'spirit of the age,' never settling or planting ourselves permanently in a community of faith. We can become too busy for God, always preoccupied and restless.

Jude describes this attitude of restlessness when he declared that the last days would be marked by people who are:

> *"**Clouds** they are without water,*
> ***carried about of winds;***

trees whose fruit withers,
without fruit, twice dead, plucked up by the roots;
raging waves of the sea,
foaming out their own shame;
wandering stars, *to whom is reserved*
the blackness of darkness for ever."
Jude 1:12-13

Waiting is not easy, **BUT IT IS THE SECRET TO STRENGTH, COURAGE AND POWER IN CHRIST!**

*"**Wait on the Lord**: be of good **courage**,*
*and He shall **strengthen your heart:***
***wait, I say, on the Lord.**"*
Psalm 27:14

God will not be rushed!

*"**GOD IS NEVER LATE...**
BUT HE NEVER COMES ON YOUR TIME."*
Bob Mumford

WAITING IS A TEST OF FAITH, OF HUMILITY AND SERVANTHOOD.

Our waiting demonstrates our dependence on God. One of the problems in a 'rush culture' is that if God doesn't do what we want when we think He should, we go out and do it ourselves!

The Importance of waiting:
The first thing that happens when we wait is that God **SIFTS** us, that is, God works on us and removes those things that would hinder and limit us on our journey of faith.

I have always been intrigued by the question: "where did the 380 disciples go to in the 10 days between the Ascension of Christ and the Day of Pentecost?" Of course, we don't know, but what we do know is they weren't there when the Holy Spirit came on the Day of Pentecost!

Power doesn't come to the impatient.

The second thing that happens to us while we wait is that God **SITUATES** us. We end up at the right place, at the right time, with the right people.

Thirdly, when we learn to wait, God **STRENGTHENS** us with His power.

"And when the Day of Pentecost had fully come…they were all filled with the Holy Spirit."
Acts 2:1-4

Finally, and most importantly, when we learn to wait, God **SEQUENCES** us. We become aligned and in tune with God's time, season and moment! We begin to activate faith in God's time and God's season.

"Knowing this first, that there shall come
*in the last days **scoffers**,*
*walking after their own **lusts**, and saying,*
***where is the promise of his coming**?*
For since the fathers died, all things continue as they
were from the beginning of the creation."
2 Peter 2:3-4

Discern the difference between God's 'moving' and God's 'moment'.

It took me a long time to work out the difference (and the gap) between God speaking and revealing something to me ('God's Moving'), and Him performing it ('God's Moment').

Like most people, I saw the two entities above as the same thing. However, years can exit between 'God's Moving' and 'God's Moment.' What do we do about it in the meantime? We have to wait! Otherwise, we get ahead of God.

When we get ahead of God, there is always a cost!

WE WILL COMPOUND OUR SPIRITUAL CONFUSION WHEN WE RUN AHEAD OF GOD.

Abraham got ahead of God – **Ishmael** was the result. (Genesis 16:1-16)

Aaron got ahead of God – people were **plagued**. (Exodus 32:35)
Joshua got ahead of God – **defeated** at Ai. (Joshua 7:1-5)
Saul got ahead of God – **rejected** by God. (1 Samuel 13:7-13)
Elijah got ahead of God – Elisha **promoted** in his place. (1 Kings 19:9-16)
Peter got ahead of God – Jesus **rebuked** his impatience. (John 18:10-11)

MEDITATIONS:

ACTIONS:

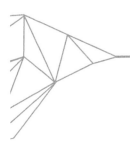

CHAPTER 5

PERSONAL TESTIMONY

"And they overcame him (the devil) by the blood of
Lamb and the Word of their testimony."
Revelations 12:11

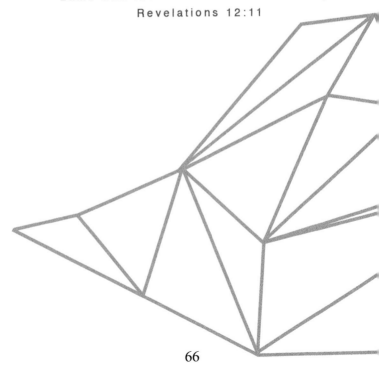

PSALM 124

"OVERCOMING BY PERSONAL EXPERIENCE"

"If it had not been the Lord who was on our side..."
Psalm 124:1

The Psalmist has made significant progress – the language and tone of the Songs has changed:
From, "In my distress I cried to the Lord."
To, "...the Lord who was on our side."

He no longer looks at a past of pain and bondage, he now sees a past of salvation and deliverance to create hope for a bright future!

He has come to know the Lord **THROUGH PERSONAL EXPERIENCE.**

He has accumulated a personal and shared history of God coming through for him and now possesses **A STORY**, which empowers him as a **WITNESS** to the Lord's saving power.

We are called to be **LIVING TESTIMONIES**, not opinionists, complainers, judges or apologists...
WITNESSES!

"But you shall receive power,
after that the Holy Spirit has come upon you:
*and you shall **BE WITNESSES** unto me..."*
Acts 1:8

"That you may be blameless and harmless,
the sons of God, without rebuke,
in the midst of a crooked and perverse nation,
among whom you SHINE AS LIGHTS in the world;
Holding forth the word of life..."
Philippians 2:15-16

We all possess a story of faith and victory, and we overcome through personal experience!

THERE IS POWER IN WHAT YOU KNOW

Notice how his journey is **CORPORATE** - "**OUR** side."

We travel as '**JOINT PILGRIMS**' along with the '**ONES WHO GO TO THE HOUSE OF GOD**,' for **OUR** experience is the same!

*"...And confessed that **they** were strangers and **pilgrims** on the earth."*
Hebrews 11:13

"Many are the afflictions of the righteous:
*but the Lord **delivers** him **out of them all**."*
Psalm 34:19

As we journey, we are accumulating our own story of God's blessings and provisions personally… I was there! It happened to me! This is my story!

A PERSON WITH AN EXPERIENCE IS NEVER SUBJECT TO A PERSON WITH A THEORY.

"Count Your Blessings" - Johnson Oatman, Jr
When upon life's billows you are tempest-tossed,
When you are discouraged, thinking all is lost,
Count your many blessings;
name them one by one,
And it will surprise you what the Lord has done.

MEDITATIONS:

ACTIONS:

70

CHAPTER 6

TRUST

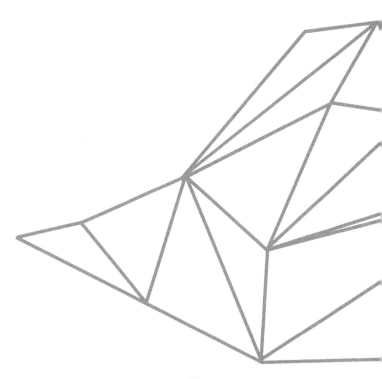

PSALM 125

"BECOMING
ESTABLISHED IN GOD"

*"Those who trust in the Lord are like Mount Zion,
which cannot be moved, but abides forever."*
Psalm 125:1

There are **three essential miracles** that must happen
in the believer if we are to progress in God.

Each 'miracle' has a **catalyst** through which the
miracle happens and marks a clear step upwards in
our journey of faith:

1. The miracle of '**ENTRANCE**' through the **NEW
    BIRTH** (repentance and faith).

    The New Birth is the first miracle where the
    new believer is supernaturally "born of God".
    This experience introduces the believer to a life
    in the spirit. Jesus explained it this way:

    *"Jesus answered and said unto him,
    verily, verily, I say unto you,*
    ***Except a man be born again,
    he cannot see the kingdom of God.***
    *Nicodemus said unto him,
    how can a man be born when he is old?*

73

Can he enter the second time
into his mother's womb, and be born?
Jesus answered, verily, verily, I say unto you,
Except a man be born of water and of the Spirit,
he cannot enter into the kingdom of God.
That which is born of the flesh is flesh;
*and **that which is born of the Spirit is spirit.***
Marvel not that I said unto you,
You must be born again.
The wind blows where it wants,
and you hear the sound thereof,
but cannot tell where it comes from,
and where it goes:
*so is every one that is **born of the Spirit**."*
John 3:3-8

2.   *The miracle of* '**COMMITMENT**' *through*
      PRIORITISING *the House of God (worship and*
      fellowship):

The 'miracle of commitment' is a revelation
and an understanding, which results in the new
believer being committed to God's House:

*"And they **continued steadfastly** in the apostles'*
*doctrine and **fellowship**,*
and in breaking of bread, and in prayers."
Acts 2:42

*"And they, **continuing daily***
*with one accord in the **temple**,*

74

*and breaking bread from **house to house,***
did eat their food with gladness
and singleness of heart,
praising God, and having favour with all the people.
*And the Lord added to the **church** daily*
those who were being saved."
Acts 2:46-47

3.   The miracle of '**ESTABLISHING**' through
     TRUST in God:

"As the Father has loved me, so have I loved you:
***continue** in my love.*
If you keep my commandments,
*you shall **abide** in my love;*
even as I have kept my Father's commandments,
*and **abide** in his love."*
John 15:9-10

The 'miracle of establishing' is the gift of strength to
continue and persevere through trust in God.

Moving from 'Faith' to 'Trust'.

This 'Song of Ascent' is a major shift in gear. It likens
the believer who "***trusts in the Lord***" to "***Mount Zion,
which cannot be removed***".

This describes the Christian who has taken the step
from '**FAITH TO TRUST**' and has become resolute,
unshakable and **UNMOVABLE**. As a result, we

become **ESTABLISHED IN GOD**!

When we are '**trusting**,' we are **calm**; we're **not anxious**; we are **settled**.

When we are '**established**,' we are **solid, settled, unmovable** and **stable** in God.

> *"If you continue in the faith **grounded and settled**, and be **not moved away** from the hope of the gospel…"*
> *Colossians 1:23*

> *"Therefore, my beloved brethren,*
> *be **steadfast, unmovable**,*
> *always abounding in the work of the Lord,*
> *for as much as you know that*
> *your labour is not in vain in the Lord."*
> *1 Corinthians 15:58*

Faith is a verb, a 'doing word'. God expects us to **act on our belief**. We begin and continue our life of faith through '**acts of obedience**'.

> *"For as the body without the spirit is dead,*
> *so **faith without works is dead** also."*
> *James 2:26*

Trust, however, is another matter altogether!

Trust is that deep, heartfelt and unshakeable

confidence in **God's nature and character**.

We develop trust in God as we progressively and personally prove God through our experiences that **He is a good, trustworthy and faithful God!**

Trust is a matter of the **heart**.

> *"Trust in the Lord with all your heart;*
> *and lean not on your own understanding.*
> *In all your ways acknowledge him,*
> *and he shall direct your paths."*
> *Proverbs 3:5-6*

The secret to **trust** is "**not leaning on our own understanding**," but trusting God totally – often in contradiction to our human understanding!

> *"For my thoughts are not your thoughts,*
> *neither are your ways my ways, says the Lord.*
> *For as the heavens are higher than the earth,*
> *so are my ways higher than your ways,*
> *and my thoughts than your thoughts."*
> *Isaiah 55:8-9*

Trust is most clearly evident when we can't act, change something, or do something about our circumstances.

**When we can't 'act on our belief',
we can still 'TRUST IN GOD.'**

In the Bible, Job offers a great example of one who trusted in God. He lost everything, and on top of that, his wife and friends were blaming and accusing him.

However, Job remained unmoved and confident because of his unwavering trust in God. In his heart, he knew God was righteous, good and just, and he refused to sin against God, even though 'logically' he would have every human reason to do so!

"Though he slay me, yet will I trust in him:
but I will maintain my own ways before him."
Job 13:15

Job kept obeying God even though the 'evidence' looked like God had deserted him.

As a young pastor, I remember responding to an invitation by our church elders to shift to Singapore (from New Zealand) with our young family for what looked to be between three to five years. We trusted God and sold all of our possessions, rented out our house and made the move with faith and excitement in our hearts.

Only eleven weeks later, we were back in New Zealand standing in an empty house thinking, "What was that all about?!" But we kept a right spirit, we stayed in church, we kept our opinions to ourselves… we trusted God!

We were able to do this because we had proved over and over that God is a good, benevolent and faithful God! We couldn't change our situation…but we could trust God. Within weeks, everything changed!

Abraham, our "father of faith", came to this same place of trust, even though all, "**human reason for hope was gone**,"

> "**In hope against hope
> Abraham believed** that he would become
> a father of many nations,
> as he had been promised [by God]:
> 'So [numberless] shall your descendants be'."
> Romans 4:18 (Amplified)

> "**When everything was hopeless,
> Abraham believed anyway**,
> deciding to live not on the basis of
> what he saw he couldn't do
> but on what God said he would do."
> Romans 4:18 (Message)

Like Job, Abraham "**believed anyway**."

Trust is "believing anyway", when there seems no reason to believe. Trust causes us to hang in there, to keep turning up, to keep moving.

When we get hurt, or disappointed in life and refuse to forgive, we have lost our trust. We may still 'believe' in

God, but we are not *"maintain(ing) our own ways before him"*. *(Job 13:15)*

The evidence that we have lost our trust in God is that we stop doing what God requires of us.

Trust is often **unseen**. It makes us unmovable, unshakeable and quietly confident that God will come through for us:

> *"For the Lord shall be your **confidence**,*
> *and shall keep your foot from being taken."*
> *Proverbs 3:26*

> *"What shall we then say to these things?*
> ***If God be for us, who can be against us**?"*
> *Romans 8:31*

The secret to maintaining trust is to never be moved from the character and **promise of God**: that He is always with us, surrounding us with His loving protection and care:

> *"As the mountains are round about Jerusalem,*
> *so **the Lord is round about his people** from*
> *henceforth even for ever."*
> *Psalm 125:2*

> *"Let your conversation be without covetousness;*
> *and be content with such things as you have:*

for he has said,
I will never leave you, nor forsake you.
So that we may boldly say,
The Lord is my helper,
and I will not fear what man shall do unto me."
Hebrews 13:5-6

MEDITATIONS:

ACTIONS:

CHAPTER 7

S O W I N G   &
R E A P I N G

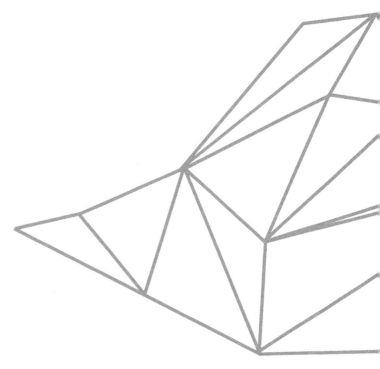

P S A L M   1 2 6

" R E S P O N D I N G   T O
A   N E W   S E A S O N "

"When the Lord turned again the captivity of Zion,
we were like them that dream.
Then our mouth was filled with laughter,
and our tongue with singing."
Psalm 126:1-2

As we journey upwards, we must take the important step of recognizing that there is a '**change in season**' **that occurs as we ascend**.

Having taken the steps of repentance, faith, prioritizing God's House, humbling ourselves as servants, experiencing God first hand and coming to a place of trust in the Lord (Psalm 120-125), we are **positioned** for the Lord to act strongly on our behalf to "***turn again our captivity***."

When the Lord '**turns the tide**' of our circumstances, like the Psalmist, we also are "filled with":

1. "**Laughter**" – filled with the '**joy** of the Lord'
2. "**Singing**" – filled with **praise** and **worship**

This "Song of Ascent" is a pivoting point in our journey of faith. The first six 'Songs of Ascent' are all about God's work '**IN**' us, where we are changed and begin our Ascent into God.

Now, in Psalm 126, there is a **change in the language**; there is a **change in the stance we are to take.**

Put simply...

We must act *with* God!

To progress further in our 'journey of Ascent,' we must be in tune and in sync with God's timing and seasons. This means we are not passive, but ready to act in unison with God.

We have become '**SOWERS**' **in God's economy and work.**

We are 'CONTRIBUTORS' AND 'PRODUCERS'!

> *"They that **sow** in tears shall **reap** in joy.*
> *He that goes forth and weeping,*
> ***bearing precious seed**,*
> *shall doubtless come again with rejoicing,*
> ***bringing his sheaves with him**."*
> *Psalm 126:5-6*

We become part of our own answer, producers of our own harvest, success and blessing!

We become **"PARTNERS," "LABOURERS" and "FELLOW WORKERS WITH GOD."**

> *"So then neither is he that **plants** any thing,*
> *neither he that **waters**;*
> *but God that gives the increase.*
> *Now he that **plants** and he that **waters** are one:*
> *and every man shall receive his own reward*
> *according to his own **labour**.*
> *For we are **labourers together** with God."*
> *1Corinthians 3:7-9*

This is the most significant of revelations...

GOD'S ECONOMY IS 'SOWING AND REAPING.'

At this stage of ascent, we shift from **'receiving FROM God'**...to **'producing FOR God'**!

> *"Herein is my Father glorified,*
> *that you **bear much fruit**;*
> *so shall you be my disciples."*
> *John 15:8*

> *"You have not chosen me,*
> *but I have **chosen you**, and **ordained you**,*
> *that you should go and **bring forth fruit**,*

*and that **your fruit should remain**:*
that whatsoever you shall ask of the Father in my
name, he may give it you."
John 15:16

Becoming a 'fruitful Christian' is the will and work of God, which requires our cooperation and participation **WITH GOD**!

"That you might walk worthy of the Lord
unto all pleasing,
being fruitful in every good work,
and increasing in the knowledge of God."
Colossians 1:10

Our journey of faith begins with God's gifts of grace **TO US** – we now progress by our gifts (seeds of faith) given back **TO HIM** to produce a harvest of righteousness.

"Now may He who supplies seed to the sower
and bread for food,
supply & multiply your seed for sowing,
and increase the fruits of your righteousness."
2 Corinthians 9:10

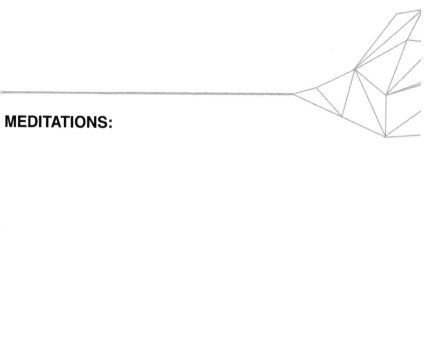

MEDITATIONS:

ACTIONS:

CHAPTER 8

BUILDERS
& KEEPERS

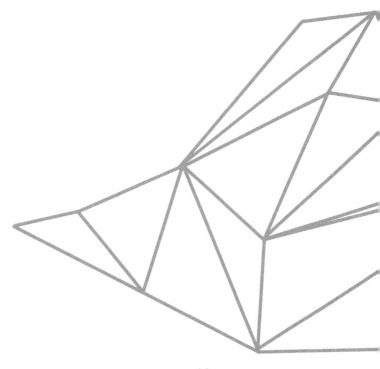

PSALM 127

"BUILDERS AND KEEPERS"

"Except the Lord build the house,
they labour in vain that build it:
except the Lord keep the city,
the watchman wake but in vain."
Psalm 127:1

The first six Songs of Ascent describe how we have become 'established' in God, and then in Psalm 126 we take the step of learning how to sustain ourselves in God's economy through sowing and reaping.

Now in this eighth Song of Ascent, we take the next vital step up to become **BUILDERS** of the House of God and **KEEPERS** of the City of God for the next generations.

We are not just '**IN**' the House of God; we are '**FOR**' the House of God!

To us, the House of God is no longer just about belonging; it's all about building, keeping, working and contributing to **make God's House great**!

"*Children are the **heritage** of the Lord*", explains the shift, as we are no longer concerned about 'our inheritance' (what we receive); we are now more concerned about the "Lord's heritage" (what the Lord receives).

We have become *"laborers together with God."* (1 Corinthians 3:9)

'**Heritage**' is simply **taking others with us** on the journey of ascent.

We have progressed from '**my need**' ("in my distress"), to '**His need**', and have become a "**Builder and Keeper**" for future generations to come!

A '**Builder**' is working and laboring **to lift others up and establish them** on the journey of Ascent.

A '**Keeper**' is **a guardian and protector** of truth and of the faith of those God has entrusted to them.

WHAT ARE OUR REWARDS?
Firstly, we are promised that "***sons and daughters***" of the same heart and mind will journey with us 'to Zion'. (Psalm 127:3-5)

Our true '**fruitfulness**' is not measured by what we '**procure**', but rather by what we '**produce**'. That is, '**sons and daughters in the faith**' – converts born and established in the House of God, our local church family.

Secondly, we shall "***never be ashamed***" before our

enemies because we are surrounded by trusted sons and daughters who will walk with us and 'fight for us'.

"Happy is the man whose quiver
is full of them (children)…"
Psalm 127:5

"But I trust in the Lord Jesus to send
Timothy shortly unto you,
that I also may be of good comfort,
when I know your state.
For I have no man likeminded,
who will naturally care for your state.
For all seek their own,
not the things which are Jesus Christ's.
But you know the proof of him,
*that, **as a son with the father,***
***he has served with me in the gospel**.*
Therefore I hope to send him presently,
so soon as I shall see how it will go with me."
Philippians 2:19-22

MEDITATIONS:

ACTIONS:

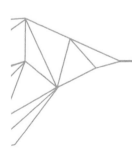

CHAPTER 9

BLESSINGS OF MATURITY

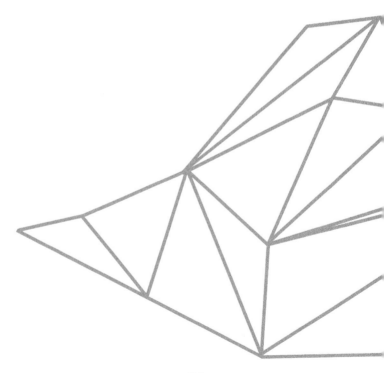

P S A L M   1 2 8

" T H E   B L E S S I N G S
O F   M A T U R I T Y "

"Blessed is every one that fears the Lord;
that walks in his ways.
For you shall eat the labour of your hands:
happy shall you be, and it shall be well with you"
Psalm 128:1

This Song presents another step up into a higher level
of spiritual progress... '**MATURITY**.'

All those who have gone before on the journey of
Ascent have built a life of **fruitfulness** and **blessing**.

This is God's heart desire and plan for us – to reach
a level of spirituality that expresses the father heart
of God. Desiring that we would be **favoured** and
blessed abundantly as His children. This has been
His plan **from the beginning**:

"So God created man in his own image,
in the image of God created he him;
male and female created he them.
*And God **blessed them**, and God said unto them,*
*Be **fruitful**, and **multiply**,*
and replenish the earth, and subdue it:
*and have **dominion** over the fish of the sea,*

and over the fowl of the air,
and over every living thing
that moves upon the earth."
Genesis 1:27-28

"BLESSED" = being fruitful, multiplying and having dominion.

The Scriptures reveal that every man and woman of God was "**BLESSED**" by God.

*"Blessed be the **God** and **Father** of our Lord Jesus Christ, who has **blessed us** with all spiritual blessings in heavenly places in Christ."*
Ephesians 1:3

We have passed the **tests** and **trials** of life and circumstances, and have been proven **faithful**!

"His lord said unto him,
*Well done, good and **faithful servant**:*
*you have been **faithful** over a few things,*
I will make you ruler over many things:
*enter into the **joy** of your lord."*
Matthew 25:21

And the Psalmist declares now that:

"...you will eat the labour of your hands:
happy shall you be, and it shall be well with you."
Psalm 128:2

The Apostle John states the same purpose at the end of the Bible...

> *"Beloved, I wish **above all things***
> *that you may **prosper** and be in **health**,*
> *even as your **soul prospers**."*
> *3 John 1:2*

God's image of us is **mature**, **complete** and **perfect** in Christ!

> *"To whom God would make known*
> *what is the riches of the glory*
> *of this mystery among the Gentiles;*
> *which is **Christ in you**, the hope of glory:*
> *Whom we preach, warning every man,*
> *and teaching every man in all wisdom;*
> *that we may **present every man***
> ***perfect in Christ Jesus**."*
> *Colossians 1:27-28*

> *"...**mature (full-grown, fully initiated, complete,***
> ***and perfect) in Christ...**"*
> *Colossians 1:28 (AMP)*

Notice that now we are mature, there is a change in language from "**children**" (Psalm 127:3), to "**children's children**"...both **natural and spiritual**.

Spiritual maturity leads to multi-generational blessing and influence.

"Now also when I am old and grey headed,
O God, forsake me not;
until I have shown your strength
unto this generation,
*and Your power t**o every one that is to come**."*
Psalm 71:18

"I will sing of the mercies of the Lord for ever:
with my mouth will I make known
*your faithfulness **to all generations**."*
Psalm 89:1

MEDITATIONS:

ACTIONS:

CHAPTER 10

PERSEVERANCE

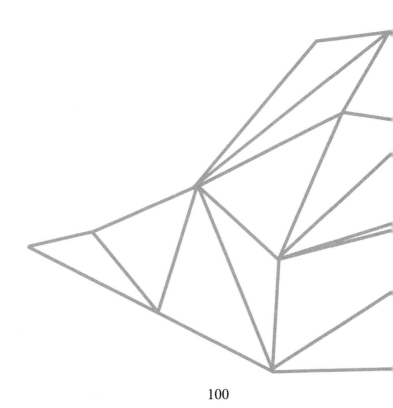

P S A L M   1 2 9

" D E V E L O P I N G   A
P E R S E V E R I N G   S P I R I T "

"Many times they have afflicted me from my youth up.
Let Israel now say,
many times they have afflicted me from my youth up,
yet they have not prevailed against me."
Psalm 129:1-2

The Psalmist declares the reality of his journey
and experiences of following the Lord...affliction,
opposition and persecution!

"Beloved, think it not strange concerning the fiery trial
which is to try you,
as though some strange thing happened unto you:
But rejoice, inasmuch as ye are partakers of Christ's
sufferings;
that, when his glory shall be revealed,
you may be glad also with exceeding joy.
If you are reproached for the name of Christ,
happy are you;
for the spirit of glory and of God rests upon you:
on their part he is spoken evil of,
but on your part he is glorified.
1Peter 4:12-14

The Lord Jesus Christ declared that we will face

opposition in this life because of our alignment with righteousness.

> *"Blessed are those who have been*
> *persecuted for righteousness' sake,*
> *for theirs is the Kingdom of Heaven.*
> *Blessed are you when people reproach you,*
> *persecute you, and say all kinds of evil*
> *against you falsely, for my sake.*
> *Rejoice, and be exceedingly glad,*
> *for great is your reward in heaven.*
> *For that is how they persecuted the prophets*
> *who were before you.*
> *Matthew 5:10-12*

The amazing thing is that as we read this Song of Ascent we discover that the Psalmist is not surprised, discouraged or disappointed at all! But rather, he is triumphant, courageous and resolute – the exact opposite to what we would expect. Surely affliction, opposition and persecution would crush us and leave us in despair? Not for those who are on the journey of ascent!

They find the strength of spirit that comes from the Lord because He acts continuously and powerfully on behalf of those who trust Him and brings to nothing the intentions and works of all opposition!

This changes our whole perspective on things.

"The Lord is righteous:
he has cut asunder the cords of the wicked."
Psalm 129:4

The apostle Peter shares this new perspective about
the "trial of our faith":

"That the trial of your faith,
being much more precious than of gold that perishes,
though it be tried with fire,
might be found unto praise and honour and glory at
the appearing of Jesus Christ"
1 Peter 1:7

What we discover is that as far as God is concerned,
it is never about the affliction, opposition or
persecution, it is always about what is produced in us
as **we go through the trial!**

"Fear not, for I have redeemed you;
I have called you by your name;
You are Mine.
When you pass through the waters,
I will be with you;
And through the rivers,
they shall not overflow you.
When you walk through the fire,
you shall not be burned,
Nor shall the flame scorch you.
Isaiah 43:1-2

Through our trials, God is building within us the most important trait that is essential for us to take the next step to ascend in our journey to God – '**perseverance**'.

Perseverance comes from having a right perspective. Perspective is seeing things from God's viewpoint.

When we come to that place and see with God's eyes, we agree with the Psalmist:

> *"Many a time have they afflicted me from my youth:*
> *Yet they have not prevailed against me!"*
> *Psalm 129:2*

In other words, it's never about our '**position**', it's all about our '**perspective**.'

> *"We know that all things work together for good to them that love God,*
> *to them who are the called according to his purpose."*
> *Romans 8:28*

This is the power of 'Stickability' – when we persevere, we **KEEP TURNING UP!**

MEDITATIONS:

ACTIONS:

CHAPTER 11

HOPE

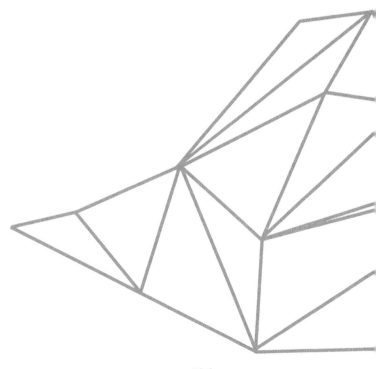

PSALM 130

"BECOMING THE ETERNAL OPTIMIST"

"Out of the depths have I cried unto You, O Lord.
Lord, hear my voice:
let Your ears be attentive
to the voice of my supplications.
If You, Lord, should mark iniquities,
O Lord, who shall stand?
But there is forgiveness with You,
that You might be feared."
Psalm 122:1

On his ascending path to Zion, the Psalmist comes to a new place, a place of hope.

This optimistic condition of heart arises from the depths of knowing God over time. It is no shallow or easy appreciation. It is the 'declaration of hope' from the heart that has confirmed and proved God's faithfulness and steadfastness over time.

"Out of the depths have I cried unto you."
Psalm 130:1

The Apostle Paul also came to this conclusion when he declared:

"And we know that all things work together for good
to them that love God,
to them who are the called
according to his purpose."
Romans 8:28

Every struggle, insecurity and sense of lack has gone and the pilgrim is now able to see himself in the light of God's perfection, forgiveness and grace, leaving him with only one conclusion – "IT'S ALL GOOD!"

"If You, Lord, should mark iniquities,
O Lord, who shall stand?
But there is forgiveness with You,
that You might be feared."
Psalm 130:3

The Psalmist began his journey with no 'depth' in himself, only desperation and need. Now there is a depth of faith, of understanding and relationship with God. He is filled with hope!

"Now may the God of hope
fill you with all joy and peace in believing,
that you may abound in hope
by the power of the Holy Spirit."
Romans 13:13

*"I **wait** for the Lord, my soul **waits**,*
*and in his word do I **hope**.*
My soul waits for the Lord

more than they that watch for the morning:
I say, more than they that watch for the morning.
*Let Israel **hope in** the Lord."*
Psalm 130:5-7

The Psalmist repeats five times that he "waits and hopes" in the Lord! This is the 'depth' to which he is referring...**GOD WILL COME THROUGH FOR ME!**

"But those who wait (hope) upon the Lord
shall renew their strength;
they shall mount up with wings as eales;
they shall run, and not be weary;
and they shall walk and not faint."
Isaiah 40:31

MEDITATIONS:

ACTIONS:

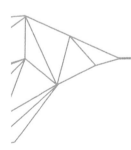

CHAPTER 12

HUMILITY

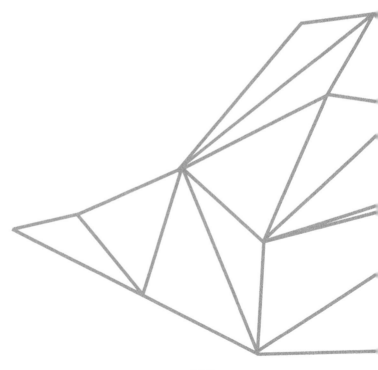

P S A L M   1 3 1
" D I S C O V E R I N G   O U R S E L V E S "

"Lord, my heart is not haughty,
nor mine eyes lofty:
neither do I exercise myself in great matters,
or in things too high for me."
Psalm 131:1

As the Psalmist is making his journey of ascent, he is coming to a place of maturity. Every step of faith is a step of progress, growth and maturity. As he takes this next step, God works in him the true mark of maturity – humility.

Humility is simply having a correct and realistic evaluation of one's self, gifts and sphere of influence. A humble person knows their place in the scheme of things.

Humility causes us to be secure and confident because we are settled and at peace with who we are. We are "bien dans sa peau," or "happy in our own skin," as the French put it.

Humility is neither 'inflated' nor 'deflated'. The Psalmist identifies the two enemies of humility as pride that 'inflates' ("my heart is not haughty") and dependency that 'deflates' *("my soul is even as a weaned child").*

The Apostle Paul described humility as "**sober thinking**," when he exhorted the Romans to not get ahead of themselves and fall into the trap of beginning to "think of themselves more highly than they ought to think":

> *"For I say, through the grace given unto me,*
> *to every man that is among you,*
> *not to think of himself more highly*
> *than he ought to think;*
> *but to think soberly,*
> *according as God has dealt to every man*
> *the measure of faith."*
> *Romans 12:3*

There are special gifts and insights to the humble because their "boast is in the Lord," not in themselves.

> *"My soul shall make its boast in the Lord:*
> *the humble shall hear of it and be glad."*
> *Psalm 34:2*

MEDITATIONS:

ACTIONS:

CHAPTER 13

OBEDIENCE

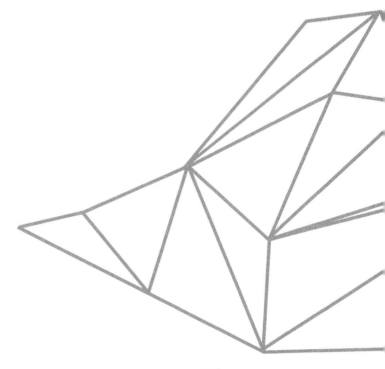

PSALM 132

"FULFILLING OUR VOW TO BUILD GOD'S HOUSE"

"For the Lord has chosen Zion;
he has desired it for his habitation.
This is my rest forever:
here will I dwell; for I have desired it."
Psalm 132:13-14

It is unclear who wrote this Psalm. Many agree that it was probably not written by David and could have been written by Solomon when he built God's House in Jerusalem. Alternatively, it may have been written by Ezra or Nehemiah when they rebuilt the temple 450 years later.

"Lord, remember David and all his afflictions:" (Psalm 132:1)

This Psalm was included and placed near the end of the fifteen Songs of Ascent because it declares the Psalmist's commitment to fulfill his vow, like David, to build God's House and find a resting place for God and His ark in His desired place, "Zion, the Mountain of the Lord."

"Lord, remember David, and all his afflictions:
How he swore unto the Lord,

and vowed unto the mighty God of Jacob;
Surely I will not come into the tabernacle of my house,
nor go up into my bed;
I will not give sleep to my eyes,
or slumber to my eyelids,
Until I find out a place for the Lord,
a habitation for the mighty God of Jacob."
Psalm 132:1-5

From the very beginning, God's House has always included three core components:

1. **Person** – the building of God's House is for God alone and His glory. We live for and serve a divine person, not a thing, concept or idea! The House of God is where God personally dwells, rests and reveals Himself on earth.

   "Unto Him be glory in the church by Christ Jesus throughout all ages, world without end. Amen."
   Ephesians 3:21

2. **Presence** – the building of God's House is for the revealing of the presence and glory of God amongst His people.

   "The house was filled with a cloud, even the house of the Lord, so that the priests could not stand to minister by reason of the cloud: for the glory of Lord filled the house of God."
   2 Chronicles 5:13-14

3.   **People** – the building of God's House is for the
        benefit and blessing of God's people.

> *"The Lord bless you out of Zion…"*
> *Psalm 128:5*

4.   **Place** – the building of God's House is for the
        creation of a practical and physical 'divine
        space' as a testimony within the human
        landscape. The physical presence of
        a dedicated House of God within the
        'architectural landscape' of a community
        cannot be underestimated. The physical
        presence of the Church within a community
        sends a message in itself that is powerful.

> *"The house that is to be built for the Lord*
> *must be exceedingly magnificent,*
> *of fame and of glory throughout all countries."*
> *1 Chronicles 22:5*

Eight Blessings in the House of God

In verses 15-18 the Psalmist declares the eight
blessings in God's House that come upon His people:

1.   *"I will abundantly bless her **provision**."*
2.   *"I will satisfy her poor with **bread**."*
3.   *"I will also clothe her priests with **salvation**."*
4.   *"Her saints shall shout aloud for **joy**."*
5.   *"There will I make the horn of David to **bud**."*
6.   *"I have ordained a **lamp** for mine anointed."*

7. *"His enemies will I clothe with **shame**."*
8. *"But upon himself shall his crown **flourish**."*

It is in the House of God, the Church, where the saints are gathered, that the fullness of God's blessings are revealed and experienced. The truth is we don't 'have it all' as individuals; the fullness of God is found in the House of God together!

> *"And (Jesus) has put all things under his feet,*
> *and gave him to be the head over all things*
> *to the church, which is his body,*
> *the fulness of him that fills all in all."*
> *Ephesians 1:22-23*

PRAYER

Heavenly Father,
I commit myself to building your House
spiritually and physically and making it great
in our community.
I promise this to Youfor Your glory
and Your pleasure alone.
Strengthen me in this resolve.

In Jesus' name,
AMEN

MEDITATIONS:

ACTIONS:

CHAPTER 14

UNITY

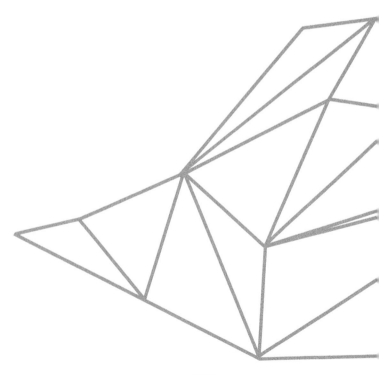

PSALM 133
"THE POWER OF UNITY"

*"Behold, how good and how pleasant it is
for brethren to dwell together in unity!
It is like the precious ointment upon the head,
that ran down upon the beard, even Aaron's beard:
that went down to the skirts of his garments;
As the dew of Hermon,
and as the dew that descended
upon the mountains of Zion:
for there the Lord commanded the blessing,
even life for evermore."
Psalm 133:1-3*

At the end of the Psalmist's journey, he has finally arrived in Zion and discovers the blessings of "dwelling in unity" in the community of faith.

This is the context into which God has been leading him, to stand on Mount Zion, shoulder to shoulder, heart to heart in unity with God's people in the House of God.

Something deep and spiritual begins to unfold in this place of unity; the anointing oil begins to flow down on leadership to permeate the whole body.

The Psalmist, along with his brothers, discovers the

'corporate anointing' – a full and all embracing.
anointing that is only revealed and experienced by
God's people who are in unity.

"…which is His body,
the fullness of Him that fills all in all."
Ephesians 1:23

Up until now, the blessings of God have been
increasingly revealed and freely bestowed upon the
pilgrim as he takes the progressive journey of faith.
Now, a whole new level of blessing is revealed – the
"**COMMANDED BLESSING**," which is only given to
those who have discovered the 'anointing of unity.'

God finds great delight and takes pleasure in this...
"Behold, how good and how pleasant it is for brethren
to dwell together in unity."

The same experience is observed on the Day of
Pentecost. God's people were in unity and the
'anointing' of the Holy Spirit fell on all of them.

Pentecost is a corporate anointing, not just a personal
experience!

"And when the day of Pentecost was fully come,
they were all with one accord in one place.
And suddenly there came a sound from heaven
as of a rushing mighty wind,
and it filled all the house where they were sitting.

*And there appeared unto them cloven tongues
like as of fire, and it sat upon each of them.
And they were all filled with the Holy Spirit,
and began to speak with other tongues,
as the Spirit gave them utterance."*
Acts 2:1-4

The Apostle Paul exhorts that once we have located
this unity, we are to do everything in our power to
"keep the unity of the Spirit…"

*"…with all lowliness and meekness,
with longsuffering, forbearing one another in love;*
endeavouring to keep the unity of the Spirit
in the bond of peace."
Ephesians 4:2-3

The 'Corporate Anointing'

This 'special anointing' is found in the experience
and atmosphere of unity and is likened to the
"**precious ointment**," or holy anointing oil, used in the
Tabernacle of Moses.

The effects of this anointing are all encompassing.
This anointing is found "**upon the head**," referring
to the anointing that rests on leadership, runs "down
upon the beard, even Aaron's beard" and "**down
to the skirts of his garments**." The whole body is
touched and influenced by this anointing.

This anointing is also likened to **"the dew of Hermon"** which comes heavily upon the mountain of Zion. All the land is completely covered with thick dew. Dew is a symbol of refreshing, quickening and invigoration.

"It is profitable as well as pleasing;
it brings blessings numerous as the drops of dew.
It cools the scorching heat of men's passions,
as the dews cool the air and refresh the earth.
It moistens the heart,
and makes it fit to receive the good seed of the word,
and to make it fruitful."
(Matthew Henry)

The Psalmist discovers the vitality, encouragement and power that comes from living in unity within a community. We are better together!

It is in this place of divine favour that God *"commands the blessing, even life for evermore."*

MEDITATIONS:

ACTIONS:

CHAPTER 15

BLESSING

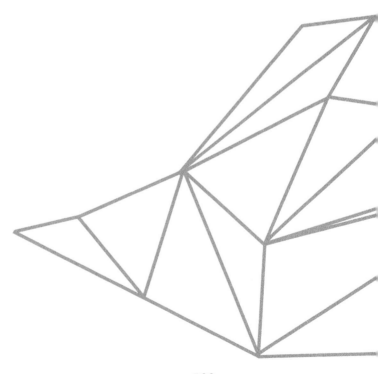

PSALM 134

"STANDING IN GOD'S HOUSE OF BLESSING"

"Behold, bless the Lord, all you servants of the Lord,
who stand by night in the house of the Lord.
Lift up your hands in the sanctuary,
and bless the Lord.
The Lord that made heaven and earth
bless you out of Zion."
Psalm 134:1-3

The Songs of Ascent conclude the journey of faith with fellow servants standing in the House of God, blessing, praising and honouring the Lord.

This is our highest calling, privilege and goal: to be a worshipper of God.

The ultimate goal of our ascent is not a 'self improvement program' or 'ministry'; it is to stand in God's House having completed our ascent, satisfied in Christ alone with our hands raised, blessing our God who made it all possible.

The imagery of this Psalm is so powerful. The servants are standing in God's House where their Spiritual ascent is complete. They are pillars, steadfast, strong, and empowered, and have overcome through every step in the journey of ascent into God's House.

This ultimate Psalm of Ascent opens exclaiming, emphasizing and drawing our attention to the word; "Behold!" (Variously translated; "Attention! (NET)"; "Look!" (WEB).

After the long journey of ascent, with all its challenges, difficulties and moments of discipleship, what do we behold? The true servants of God standing together in God's House "blessing the Lord!"

This short, final song pictures a trilogy of "blessing" (blessing God twice and blessing servants once):

"Behold, bless the Lord,
All you servants of the Lord,
Who by night stand in the house of the Lord!
Lift up your hands in the sanctuary,
And bless the Lord.
The Lord who made heaven and earth
Bless you from Zion!"
Psalm 134:1-3

We behold the faithful servants of God blessing the Lord "by night," at the 'end of the day' (when all is complete). They are found in the house of God with hearts full of praise and blessing towards Him.

But this is not a 'one way street.' How can it be? For

who can out-give God? As we stand in awe of God, declaring his goodness and mercy, God responds by blessing us "out of Zion (the Church, the House of God)," just like our father of faith, Abraham:

*"The Lord that made heaven and earth
bless you out of Zion."*
Psalm 134:3

We stand in God's House not only blessing, but also blessed to be a blessing!

*"I will bless you and make your name great.
You will be a blessing."*
Genesis 12:2

This is the promise and "blessing of Abraham," to not only be blessed, but to be a blessing!

*"So then they which be of faith
are blessed with faithful Abraham."*
Galatians 3:9

*"Blessed be the God and Father
of our Lord Jesus Christ,
who has blessed us with all spiritual blessings in
heavenly places in Christ."*
Ephesians 1:3

MEDITATIONS:

ACTIONS:

SELAH

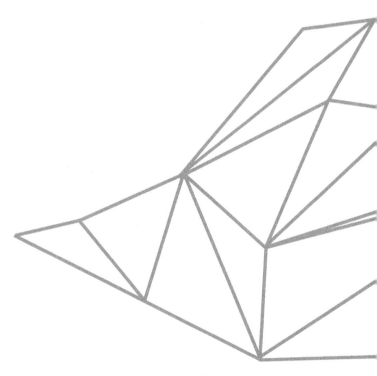